Andrew & Ashley's EUROPEAN TOURS

LONDON TRAVEL JOURNAL

THIS BOOK BELONGS TO

_____

BE SURE TO GET THE LONDON TRAVEL GUIDE FOR REFERENCE. AND DON'T MISS THE OTHER BOOKS IN THE SERIES!

SCAN ME

Get the *Andrew & Ashley's European Tours: London!* here.

LONDON TRAVEL JOURNAL

Hi there! Hope you're ready to enjoy your London tours with us. Before you go, we've got a few checklists to make sure you've got everything you need.

This London Travel Journal will be great to jot down few memories during your trip so you can look back and remember all the fun things you did. You can also share it with your friends and family when you return!

This is your official journal to write down what you see, hear, smell and taste while you are in London!

What was your favorite tour, food, experience?
What did you see that you weren't expecting?
Who did you meet?

FIRST A LITTLE PREPARATION FOR THE TRIP!

WHAT WILL I PACK ON THIS TRIP TO LONDON

Packing checklist!

Make sure to check the weather forecast before you go. It can rain and be foggy sometimes in London. Better to be ready for anything!
One of the challenges of travel is the time it takes to get there and being patient for periods of time while you wait your turn. So pack plenty of things to keep yourself busy.

ITEMs	How Many?	ITEMs	How Many?
Pants		Download movies	
Shorts (or skirts!)		Backpack	
Shirts		· Tablet	
Jacket or sweatshirts		· This travel journal!	
Rain coat with hood or a hat		· Andrew & Ashley's European Tours for London book ☺	
Hat to shade from sun			
Sunglasses			
Walking shoes (tennies)		· Andrew & Ashley's European Tours LONDON!	
Nicer shoes for going out to a play or dinner		○ London Itinerary (see page 48)	
Socks		· Pen, pencil, coloring pens	
Underwear!		· Book to read	
Pajamas		· Headphones	
Toothbrush		· Passport and IDs	

Check with an adult who is going on the trip with you for other things you might need and put them on your list above!

WHAT I NEED TO GET AROUND LONDON.

Pre-travel Checklist

An adult in your group should have this information at the ready either on their cell phone or printed out:

___ app or website with a map of the Underground

___ a taxi app on their phone

___ tickets for reserved tours with QR codes for everyone

___ itinerary or tour plan by day with location addresses and mode of transportation

___ GPS app on someone's mobile phone

___ name and address of the hotel where you're staying

___ cell and data roaming on your smart phones for the UK

TRAVEL TIPS

Many museums now have an app with an audio guide that you can load onto your cell phone. Or you can rent an audio guide at the museum. Check with your adults on how you want to handle that.

Remember, it's important to be organized to make sure you don't miss a thing! The travel time between places might be longer than you think.

Got everything "sorted" (organized)?
You're READY! Let's go travel!

TO JOG YOUR MEMORY – HERE'S A MAP OF WHERE WE'RE GOING

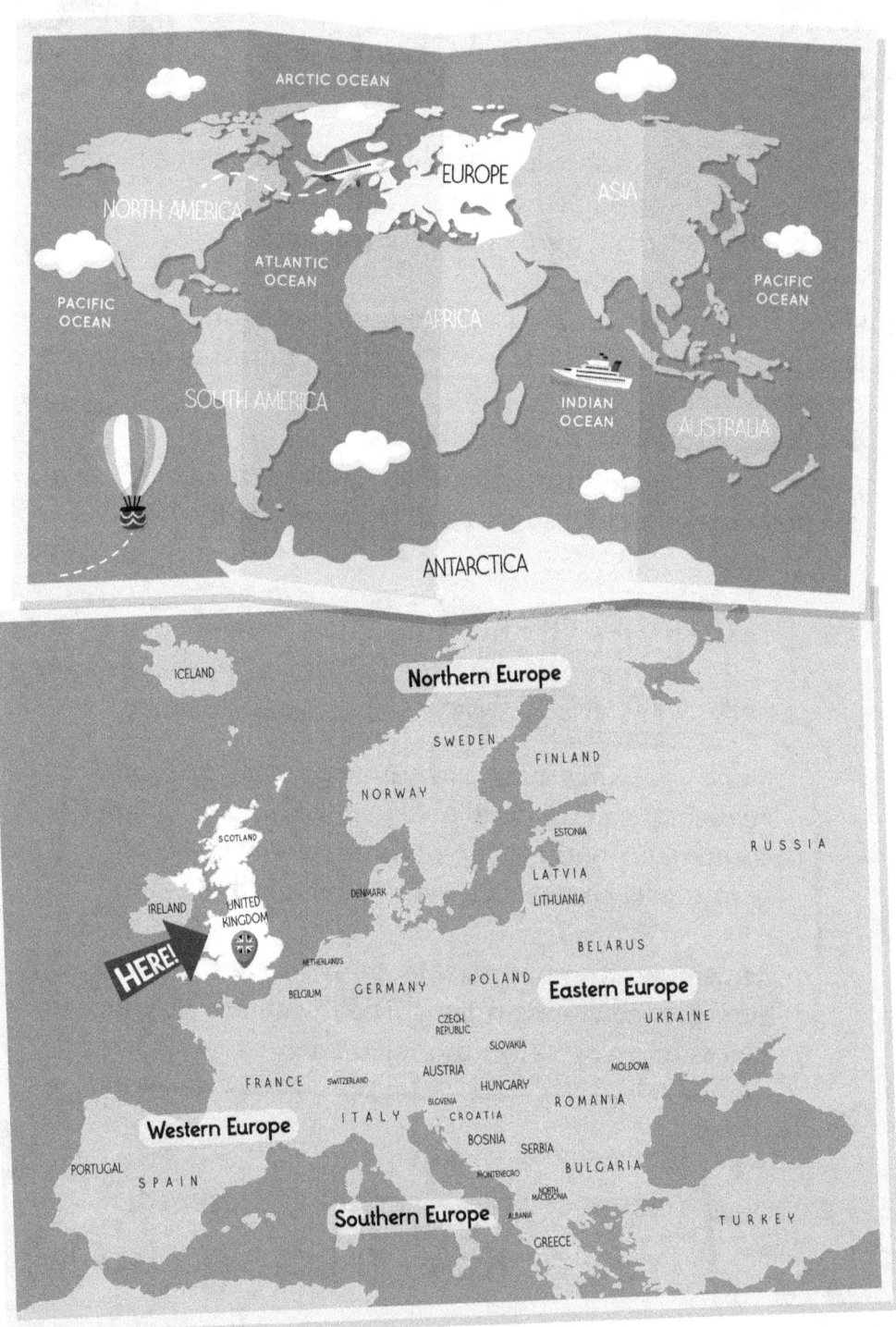

WHERE ARE YOU COMING FROM, AND HOW ARE YOU GETTING TO LONDON

My home is here:

city or town _____
state _____
country _____

This is how I will get to London:
___airplane
___car
___train
___bus
___other _____

We traveled from this city before getting to London:

_____

If you are flying, what type of airplane is it?
(Hint: you can find out in the seat front pocket guide.)

_____

London has several airports, at which one will you land?
___Gatwick
___Heathrow
___other _____

How will I get to London from the airport?
___Black Taxi
___the Underground
___app taxi
___tour bus
___train
___other _____

What hotel are you staying in, in London?

_____

LONDON TRAVEL JOURNAL

While you travel, you're going to want to write down some of the great things you've seen, heard and tasted.

Use this guide on your trip and after you return to create a record of everything. It's so nice to look back on it later!

I'm betting your friends and family will love to hear about it too.

LONDON'S FOOD CULTURE:

When you visit other countries, there will always be unique food to try. The important thing is that you try it so you know whether you want to eat it again. When you're an adult you may come back.

What was your favorite food you tried in London, or how about your least favorite?

Favorite food I tasted in London:

_____

Least favorite food I tasted in London:

_____

Did you go to lunch in a pub? What was that like?

_____

Food I tasted while in London
___fish & chips
___shepherd's pie
___cornish pasty
___scone with clotted cream
___chips
___crisps
___sunday roast
___English breakfast
___toad in the hole
___bangers and mash

LONDON'S ART CULTURE:

We hope you had time to visit the museums where so much famous art and artifacts are on display.

What was your favorite artist and painting you saw in London?

Favorite painting I saw in London:

_____

What was the artists name?

_____

Other types of art I saw:

_____

LONDON'S THEATRE CULTURE:

As we've mentioned, the plays and musicals in London are some of the best in the world. Did you go see a play or musical while in London?

Even if you didn't get the time, what do you want to see?

A play or musical I saw while in London:

_____

A play or musical I wanted to see while in London:

_____

If you were lucky enough to go to the theatre, glue or tape your ticket or a cut out from the brochure below:

LONDON'S MUSIC CULTURE:

Music is all around us in the world, but you may or may not have had time to go to a live music event or learn about musicians.

Did you go to Abbey Road or tour the studios where the famous Beatles walked and created music?

My favorite music by a British artist is:

_____

My least favorite is:

_____

If you went to Abbey Road and took a photo walking on the road or in front of the studio, glue or tape your photo here!

LONDON'S BOOKS & MOVIES CULTURE:

In Andrew & Ashley's London travel guide we listed many books that turned into movies, so much to see on this subject.

What is your favorite British book that is also a movie written by someone in the UK?

Favorite book that is also a movie, written by someone from the UK:

_____

A British book or movie I liked when I was younger, but I've moved on: 😊

_____

Draw your favorite character here, or glue or tape a picture of them:

LONDON'S SPORTS CULTURE: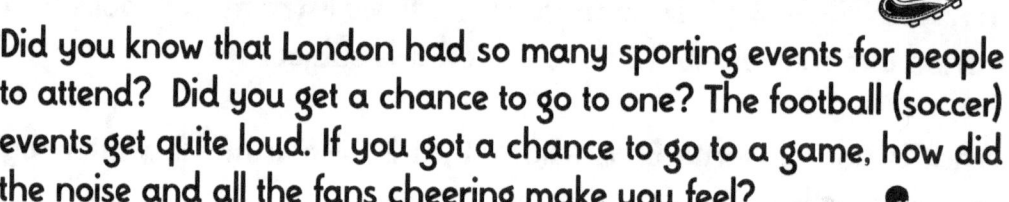

Did you know that London had so many sporting events for people to attend? Did you get a chance to go to one? The football (soccer) events get quite loud. If you got a chance to go to a game, how did the noise and all the fans cheering make you feel?

I saw a group of people wearing their team's jerseys, which teams were they?

_____

I went to a sporting event, and here's what I liked about it:

_____

My favorite professional or social sport in England is:

_____

Draw or trace your favorite sport from the book here:

LONDON'S ROYAL FAMILY CULTURE:

We hope you got a chance to learn about the royal family members. Some of William and Kate's kids are your age. Which member of the royal family is your favorite?

My favorite member of the royal family:

_____

What does this family member do that you like the most:

_____

There are a lot of people working to keep the royal family in business. What kind of jobs did you see people doing?

_____

Draw or trace your favorite royal family member from the book here:

ENGLISH YOU SAY, SIR?

Where were you when you heard someone speaking English but it didn't sound like the way you would say it?

Did it make you giggle? You can even turn on the television to hear them!

Places I heard different accents in London:

_____

_____

_____

What is your favorite word in English that Brits say a different way?

_____

Did you go to "high tea" during your visit?

Did you have "chips" while you were visiting?

Did you see any coppers?

What's the English word for garbage? _____

What do you call your friend in the UK? _____

PEOPLE I MET OR SAW WHILE I WAS IN LONDON

We try to strike up conversations with the people we meet when we travel. It makes it more fun and sometimes we find out about cool stuff going on.

Did you ask any questions or strike up a conversation with people you met? Did you meet any kids your age?

- Hotel workers
- Restaurant workers
- Tour guides
- Pilot or airline workers
- Store clerks
- Football fans
- People in a pub
- People at dinner or lunch
- Museum workers
- Theatre workers
- Other
- Other kids

- Royal family members
- Actors
- Sports people
- Models
- Other _____

Darn! I wish I would have seen someone famous, but I had fun anyway.

MY FAVORITE THINGS I LIKED ABOUT LONDON

During the whole trip, the things I liked the most was:
- the culture
- the tours
- all the forms of transportation
- the people I met
- all the accents I heard
- the museums
- the theatre
- the monuments and statues
- stories about royalty and their jewels!
- the stately homes
- learning about sports!
- other

Write about your experiences here:

Andrew and Ashley gave you a list of their top places to visit while in London. Let's start with this list - did you have any favorites here?

London Eye

Shrek's Adventure

London Dungeon

London Aquarium

London Bridge

Tower of London

The Crown Jewels

Changing of the Guard

The Shard

Borough Market

HMS Belfast World War II Ship

National Maritime Museum

Old Royal Naval College

Buckingham Palace

The Royal Mews

Westminster Abbey

The Palace of Westminster

Harry Potter tour

Windsor Castle

Natural History Museum

Theatre!

Trafalgar Square

Hyde and Kensington parks

Pick YOUR TOP 5 tours and list them on the next page!

COLOR IN LONDON

There are two famous London icons in this picture. What are they?
_____ and _____

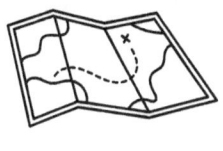

MY LONDON TRIP JOURNAL

What were my TOP 5 favorite places to visit?

FAVORITE PLACES

Visit #1: _____

Visit #2: _____

Visit #3: _____

Visit #4: _____

Visit #5: _____

Later in the book you can write in a journal page about it.
First let's find out what you liked about London in general!

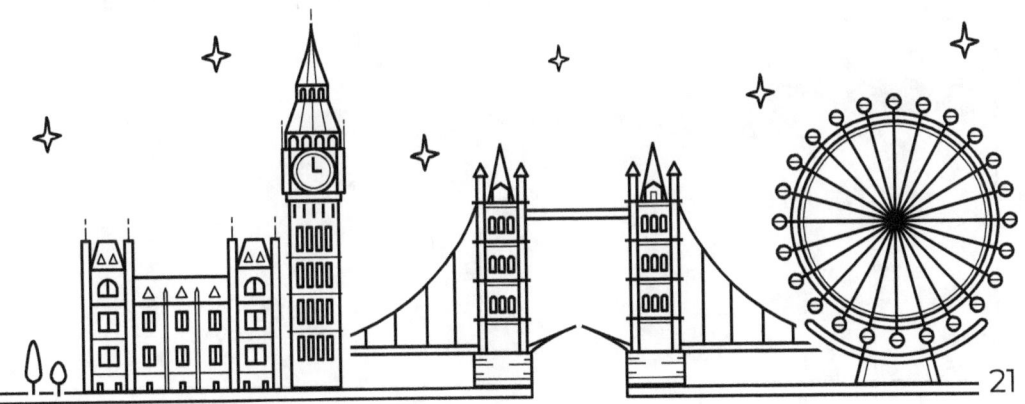

My #1 favorite visit was:

_____

It was my #1 favorite because:

_____

My favorite thing I saw was:

_____

Something I saw that I've never seen before:

_____

Who was the most famous person mentioned on this tour:

_____

The part I didn't like was:

_____

Something I'm going to tell people about when I get home is:

_____

Something I found weird or funny (and maybe kinda wonderful) about this visit:

_____

Draw, glue or tape something from your tour here:

Overall rating for this or event tour is: _____ stars

Color in the number of stars above to indicate your score!

On this tour or at this event I learned about:

- people's lives
- art
- royalty
- people's jobs
- famous people
- history
- culture
- government
- sports
- other

On this tour or at this event I heard:

- funny words
- horses
- sports fans getting excited
- music
- loud noises
- traffic sounds
- people laughing
- a tour guide talking
- an audience clapping
- other

Write in your journal in your own words what you experienced, who you met, what you liked, or didn't!

_____

_____

_____

_____

_____

_____

_____

My #2 favorite visit was:

_____

It was my #2 favorite because:

_____

My favorite thing I saw was:

_____

Something I saw that I've never seen before:

_____

Who was the most famous person mentioned on this tour:

_____

The part I didn't like was:

_____

Something I'm going to tell people about when I get home is:

_____

Something I found weird or funny (and maybe kinda wonderful)
about this visit:

_____

Draw, glue or tape something from your tour here:

Overall rating for this or event tour is: _____ stars

Color in the number of stars above to indicate your score!

On this tour or at this event I learned about:

- people's lives
- art
- royalty
- people's jobs
- famous people
- history
- culture
- government
- sports
- other

On this tour or at this event I heard:

- funny words
- horses
- sports fans getting excited
- music
- loud noises
- traffic sounds
- people laughing
- a tour guide talking
- an audience clapping
- other

Write in your journal in your own words what you experienced, and who you met, what you liked, or didn't!

_____

_____

_____

_____

_____

_____

_____

My #3 favorite visit was:

_____

It was my #3 favorite because:

_____

My favorite thing I saw was:

_____

Something I saw that I've never seen before:

_____

Who was the most famous person mentioned on this tour:

_____

The part I didn't like was:

_____

Something I'm going to tell people about when I get home is:

_____

Something I found weird or funny (and maybe kinda wonderful) about this visit:

_____

Draw, glue or tape something from your tour here:

26

Overall rating for this or event tour is: _____ stars

Color in the number of stars above to indicate your score!

On this tour or at this event I learned about:
- people's lives
- art
- royalty
- people's jobs
- famous people
- history
- culture
- government
- sports
- other

On this tour or at this event I heard:
- funny words
- horses
- sports fans getting excited
- music
- loud noises
- traffic sounds
- people laughing
- a tour guide talking
- an audience clapping
- other

Write in your journal in your own words what you experienced, and who you met, what you liked, or didn't!

_____

_____

_____

_____

_____

_____

_____

_____

My #4 favorite visit was:

_____

It was my #4 favorite because:

_____

My favorite thing I saw was:

_____

Something I saw that I've never seen before:

_____

Who was the most famous person mentioned on this tour:

_____

The part I didn't like was:

_____

Something I'm going to tell people about when I get home is:

_____

Something I found weird or funny (and maybe kinda wonderful) about this visit:

_____

Draw, glue or tape something from your tour here:

Overall rating for this or event tour is: ____ stars

Color in the number of stars above to indicate your score!

On this tour or at this event I learned about:

- people's lives
- art
- royalty
- people's jobs
- famous people
- history
- culture
- government
- sports
- other

On this tour or at this event I heard:

- funny words
- horses
- sports fans getting excited
- music
- loud noises
- traffic sounds
- people laughing
- a tour guide talking
- an audience clapping
- other

Write in your journal in your own words what you experienced, and who you met, what you liked, or didn't!

_____

_____

_____

_____

_____

_____

_____

My #5 favorite visit was:

_____

It was my #5 favorite because:

_____

My favorite thing I saw was:

_____

Something I saw that I've never seen before:

_____

Who was the most famous person mentioned on this tour:

_____

The part I didn't like was:

_____

Something I'm going to tell people about when I get home is:

_____

Something I found weird or funny (and maybe kinda wonderful)
about this visit:

_____

Draw, glue or tape something from your tour here:

Overall rating for this or event tour is: ____ stars

Color in the number of stars above to indicate your score!

On this tour or at this event I learned about:

- people's lives
- art
- royalty
- people's jobs
- famous people
- history
- culture
- government
- sports
- other

On this tour or at this event I heard:

- funny words
- horses
- sports fans getting excited
- music
- loud noises
- traffic sounds
- people laughing
- a tour guide talking
- an audience clapping
- other

Write in your journal in your own words what you experienced, and who you met, what you liked, or didn't!

_____

_____

_____

_____

_____

_____

_____

COLOR IN LONDON

Which three historical places can be found in this picture? _____, _____ and _____

JOURNAL PAGES

Write down, draw, or paste something about your trip!
Consider adding a date and what you saw, who you met,
and what you learned.

JOURNAL PAGES

Write down, draw, or paste something about your trip!
Consider adding a date and what you saw, who you met,
and what you learned.

JOURNAL PAGES

Write down, draw, or paste something about your trip!
Consider adding a date and what you saw, who you met,
and what you learned.

JOURNAL PAGES

Write down, draw, or paste something about your trip!
Consider adding a date and what you saw, who you met,
and what you learned.

www.ingramcontent.com/pod-product-compliance
Lightning Source LLC
Chambersburg PA
CBHW082113120626
46553CB00011B/3667